WHAT AM I?

VERY FIRST RIDDLES

by Stephanie Calmenson
Pictures by Karen Gundersheimer

Harper & Row, Publishers

To Jane Feder

S. C.

*To Jay and Rubens
with love*

K.G.

What Am I? Very First Riddles
Text copyright © 1989 by Stephanie Calmenson
Illustrations copyright © 1989 by Karen Gundersheimer
Printed in Singapore. All rights reserved.
1 2 3 4 5 6 7 8 9 10
First Edition

Library of Congress Cataloging-in-Publication Data
Calmenson, Stephanie.
  What am I?

  Summary: A collection of easy-to-read riddles in
verse about everyday objects.
  1. Riddles, Juvenile. [1. Riddles] I. Gundersheimer,
Karen, ill. II. Title.
PN6371.5.C325 1989   818'.5402   87-22959
ISBN 0-06-020997-6
ISBN 0-06-020998-4 (lib. bdg.)

Tick, tick, tick
Is the sound I make.
Or ring, ring, ring,
To help you wake.

What am I?

A clock.

To guess what I am
Is easy as can be.
Your sock goes on your foot
And your foot goes into me.

What am I?

A shoe.

Though we jingle and jangle,
That's not what we're for.
You need one of us
To unlock your door.

What are we?

Keys.

I ring until you pick me up.
You hold me to your ear.
Then someone who is far away
Seems to be right here.

What am I?

A telephone.

I hang from a bar,
Or sometimes a tree.
Ask a friend for a push
When you ride on me.

What am I?

A swing.

You'll find us on your birthday cake,
Each one of us aglow.
Close your eyes and make a wish,
Then take a breath and blow!

What are we?

Candles.

We're pretty to look at
And nice to smell.
If you have a garden,
You know us well.

What are we?

Flowers.

I have three wheels
And a horn to blow.
Just pedal, pedal,
Then off we go.

What am I?

A tricycle.

When rain comes falling
Down from the sky,
Open me up
If you want to stay dry.

What am I?

An umbrella.

When the rain is gone,
And the sun peeks through,
I'm the colorful surprise
That's waiting for you.

What am I?

A rainbow.

Dip the wand
And gently blow.
Off we sail,
Then POP! we go.

What are we?

Bubbles.

I have string and a tail,
And I'm made to fly.
On a breezy day,
See me up in the sky.

What am I?

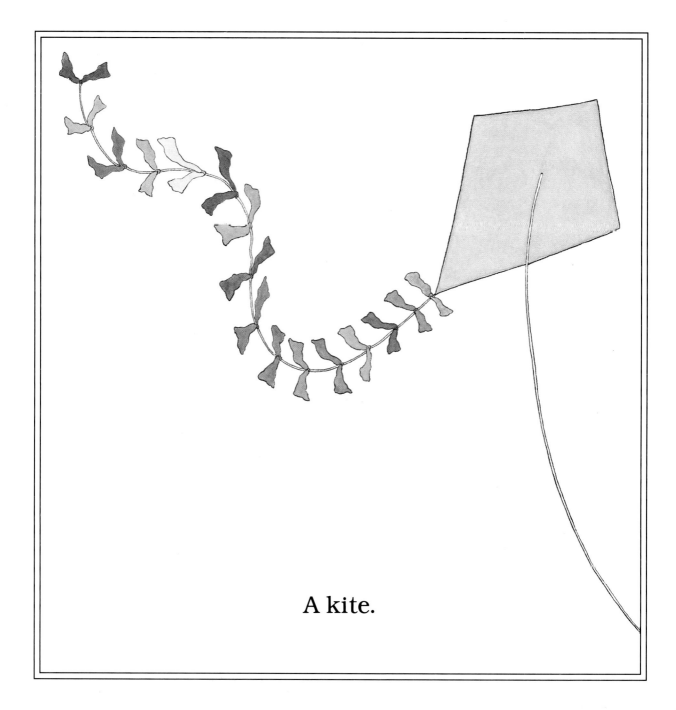

A kite.

I'm sweet and cold,

So take a lick.

But watch me melt

If you're not quick!

What am I?

Ice cream.

Listen to me! Listen to me!

Clickety-clack!

Watch for me! Watch for me!

Coming down the track.

What am I?

A train.

You're almost at the end of me.

Just one more page to go.

I hope you'll share me with a friend.

What am I? Do you know?

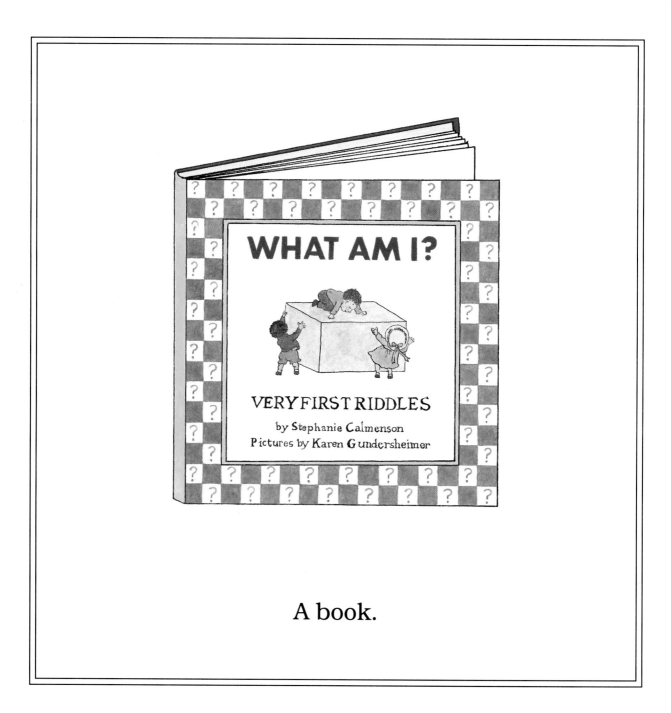

A book.